Yarns of Inspiration I

Ama Duncan
The Fabulous Woman Network

Yarns Of Inspiration I

Copyright ©2017 The Fabulous Woman Network

All rights reserved.
Written permission must be secured from the publisher to use or reproduce any part of this book, except for brief quotations in critical reviews or articles.

ISBN: 978-9988-2-5048-5

Cover Design:
Reaga Right Media Productions
+233243807152

Typesetting:
Jemimah Addy
+233208402865

Cover Photo:
Vera Obeng Photography
+233276038503

Dedication

To My Father in Heaven
To My Family
To My Friends

Acknowledgements

Jesus; you enabled me.
Samuel Duncan; you had my back.
Paris and Troy; you two have taught me valuable lessons in life.
Gladys Aba Hagan; my number one cheerleader.
Reaga Right (Kwesi Mbir); I don't always like it when you push me, but boy do I need it!
Xavier Afful; you proudly showed off my work.
Vera Ewura Obeng; you know I love the cover photo right?
Akua Bobson; you edited this book.
Jemimah Addy; you had time for my 1001 questions about publishing.
Kojo Yankson; your 'Messages From The Morning Man' inspired me to start writing again.
Dr. Isaac Quaye; you consistently gave me wise counsel.
Dr. Sybil Pentsil; you guided me.
Vera Ngo'ma and Anita Annan; you advised me.
Francisca Ampratwum and Rita Krampah; you encouraged me.
Nkechi Dike; you gave me constructive feedback.
Barima Makeup Artistry; you made my face shine.
Joseph Kyei Mensah; you said 'do it!'.
Ambrose and Ekua E. Houphouet; you supported me.
Team TFWN; you did all the hardwork!
My family and friends; you backed me!
The FWN Followers; I love serving you!

To you all and everyone who has ever sent me a kind word of encouragement, prayed or been there for me: I am forever grateful!

Contents

Dedication	3
Acknowledgements	4
Introduction	6
1. Finally, Opportunity Came Banging On My Door!	7
2. Why I Went Back To My First Love	11
3. Don't Worry; God's Got Our Backs	14
4. That Annoying Tinge Of Jealousy	16
5. Be Careful, But Of Whom?	20
6. Women Are Our Own Angels	23
7. 3-Square Meals, Snacks And Brazilian Hair	26
8. Be Fabulous, Not Judgemental	29
9. Stay Quiet And Let God Do The Talking	31
10. I Must Mirror My Fabulous Sister	34
11. Is That A Whole Box Of Prawns?	37
12. My Boots, My Right	41
13. Order From Above: Be Submissive	43
14. Simple, Fabulous And Romantic	46
15. The Dreadful Road To Bravery	48
16. The Table Or The Enemy?	52
17. Young Fabulous Woman, Wake Up And Make Your Dream A Reality!	55
18. The Mandela Way	57
19. When Jesus Says Yes…	60
20. Fabulous Woman, It's OK To Make The First Move!	63
21. Think. Pray. Eat Jollof And Move!	67
22. Glossary	76
23. Bibliography	77
24. The Author	78

Introduction

Theodore Roosevelt was not kidding when he said 'believe, and you are halfway there'. To be an Author has been a dream I have fantasized about since I was in primary school. Somehow, I saw myself as one and today I get to be called one! God has been good.

Yarns of Inspiration I, is a compilation of some of the short stories I have been sending for publication via Daily Graphic (leading Ghanaian Newspaper), www.myjoyonline.com, www.starrfmonline.com and amaduncan.com (my blog). My friend Nkechi actually coined a term for it, 'blook'; because it consists of blogs turned into a book.

In this book, I share personal experiences I have had as well as some thoughts on some of life's issues and challenges. It has been an amazing and exciting journey for me, as a new Author. I sincerely hope that you can resonate with some of the stories shared here, take inspiration from my experiences, get new ideas, and keep on moving forward. I strongly believe that you are fabulous!

Ama xx

1
Finally, Opportunity Came Banging On My Door!

I had been sailing through life without any particular purpose; I would run after any opportunity that came my way because I didn't really know what I wanted to 'be in future'. At home, I had a great life with a very supportive husband and two wonderful kids. I had completed my Master's in Human Resources Management (mostly because everyone else was getting a master's!). I was in a great career doing corporate training as well but I felt I needed to do more. There was a burning desire within me to be an inspiration to others but I just didn't know how.

In 2015, while thinking of 'what next', I knew whatever 'it' was had to involve writing because I loved reading and writing as a child. But what was I going to write about? Fashion, inspirational stories, women...wait a minute! "How about the women who inspired me as a way of celebrating them?" I thought. I mean, I got so much inspiration from women who were successful in spite of their challenges, past mistakes and fears. So why not write about them and share their stories with the rest of the world? Thus, I started writing about inspirational women and decided to go a step further by posting the articles on Facebook. With the help of Reaga Right and Setso Ziddah (two incredibly talented young men), I started a new page on Facebook called "The Fabulous

Woman," where I posted stories about such women. I loved the word 'Fabulous,' especially because of its use in Marianne Williamson's "Our Deepest Fear."

"The Fabulous Woman" was just a hobby but people who came across it thought it was amazing. We had very few followers and I used to look at pages with 1000 likes and wish ours could grow to that number. Can you imagine? My little mind just wanted 1000 likes!! Haha! Anyway, the only problem was that I didn't know how to get more traffic to the page. I kept cracking my brain on how we could get more exposure but the answer was not forthcoming. So I just kept on doing what I was doing: you know, pestering women to share stories of their lives to inspire others. My hope was that someday, we would be discovered by a 'big somebody' who would help me achieve my goal of celebrating, developing and inspiring people, especially women. I waited and waited for that opportunity. Guess what, it never came!

For me, the saying "If opportunity doesn't knock, build a door" is very true. However, it took too long for me to realize that opportunity was never going to knock because I had no apparent door. What opened my eyes to this simple truth? Here is what happened: I discovered a book called 'Rich Dad, Poor Dad.' Actually, I talk about this book so much that my friend Francisca Ampratwum once said, "You mention this book a lot. Why, is it the only book you've read?" Hahahaha! No, I have read other books but 'Rich Dad, Poor Dad' was an eye-opener for me in a lot of ways! In the book, Robert Kiyosaki (the author) told the story of a conversation with a female journalist in Singapore who was an impressive author. Yet she moaned that although people said her novels were excellent, her work did not seem to go anywhere. She said her dream was to become a bestselling author like Robert and therefore needed his advice. Robert's advice to the lady was simple: "LEARN HOW TO SELL." That was when it hit me! Of course! That explains why some people are so good but you never hear of them. We all need to learn how to market ourselves. This was a simple but extremely eye-opening revelation for me. How come I never thought of that? I mean yes, "The Fabulous Woman" idea was great but in order to impact the world, the world had to know it existed, right?

From that day forward, I decided to learn more about branding. In fact, I took Personal Branding, personal. The first book recommended to me was "Re-inventing You" by Dorie Clark, an amazing Personal Branding guru. I also read short articles on Forbes and other renowned websites about the subject. Most of them mentioned online presence, which made a lot of sense actually because these days, millions of people are online.

My biggest online presence was Facebook so that was my first point of attack. My goal was to ensure that anyone who came across my profile knew these facts about me: "I'm a child of God; I am married with kids; I love a good laugh; I love to celebrate, develop and inspire especially women and I am a Corporate Trainer." I decided from that day to take social media seriously and treat it more as an important marketing tool and less as 'just a social thing'. I got to work; opening up my doors to new connections and searching for strategic connections. Fast forward to today, people who come across my account have a clearer idea of what I'm about and I tend to attract the people who need my services. Now, opportunity is beginning to knock on my door because I finally built one. We still have a long way to go, but I am confident that this is what God needs me to do for His glory at this time and I am so humbled and grateful that He would choose me to lead this particular cause.

I am Ama Duncan, a fabulous child of God, wife, mother, Corporate Trainer and Founder of Corporate Training Solutions and The Fabulous Woman Network. Thank you for reading a bit about me. Follow us on social media (Facebook, Instagram and Twitter: The Fabulous Woman Network, www.thefabulouswomannetwork.com or www.amaduncan.com) for inspirational messages that will bless you to be a blessing.

Ama xx

2
Why I Went Back To My First Love

This story is definitely not about my childhood sweetheart, although I would love to share that confusing story with you someday. No, this is about my other love.

As a young girl, I loved to read and I would read anything I laid my hands on: romance novels, mystery stories, historical works, P&P Newspapers (I wonder if we still have those), just about any book or magazine available to a small-town girl. A number of times in school, I actually had my books seized because I was caught reading (usually a Sweet Valley High novel) while lessons were ongoing. Some adults I met even told me that I had to become a lawyer because I never got tired of reading. No, I never did...!

...Until one day when I became a busy woman. I became a busy career woman; then a busy married career woman. Shortly after that, a busy married career woman with two kids. Then a busy married career woman with two kids trying to get her Master's degree. Almost immediately after that, a busy married career woman with two kids trying to get her Master's degree and do 'kpakpakpa' business. Surely, I would not have time for reading, right? Those were my excuses and I defended them with vigor.

Yarns Of Inspiration I

Well, I finally finished my MBA in Human Resources Management but everything else remained the same except for one thing: I was tired of being broke all the time. I yearned for financial independence. I became tired of cringing with fear and disappointment every time someone asked me for financial help and I knew I could not help. This made me sad and miserable. I just did not know what to do to gain financial independence. It was not as if I owed people, I just wanted to be able to have the money I had earned in order to spend the way I wanted to, aside from my normal motherly/wifely responsibilities.

One day, my daughter, who was then six years old, picked up a book which had been lying around the house for well over two years. I asked her to get another book more suited to her age but she insisted on reading that book. I decided to let her. We were on our way out, so while I started the car I asked her, 'What did you learn from the book?' She replied ever-so-nonchalantly, 'Well, the book said poor people work for money while rich people let their money work for them.' I slammed the brakes as a light bulb went off in my head. But of course, this was exactly why I was not rich! I kept working for money instead of letting money work for me! So had I been doing it wrong all this time? I wondered how I could miss this simple truth. The book 'Rich Dad, Poor Dad' had been lying in my house for over two years. Why had I not read it? In fact, why on earth did I ever stop reading in the first place? How could I ignore the fact that successful people invested in reading?

Why I Went Back To My First Love

With these words of wisdom coming from the innocent lips of a six-year old who had no idea how her words had affected me, I vowed to start reading again. I realized that if I was ever going to be successful at achieving financial independence, I had to go back to my first love: reading. And oh, I fell right back in love with reading, as if I had never left.

I would love to tell you that I am richer now but no, I am not. However, with each book, article, Dave Ramsey or Ted video I watch, I move a step closer to my dream. Hopefully someday soon, I will be rich but I will keep reading while waiting! And guess what, I am still a married career woman with two kids and three budding businesses. Yet, now I find time to read and even write (my second love) occasionally because I am simply in love. Love does move mountains! Recently, I told a friend that I become sad when I get sleepy because I don't want to stop reading. She looked at me incredulously saying, 'I don't understand why you read when you can watch The Wendy Williams Show!' Haha, I guess we all have what makes us happy!

My fabulous sisters and brothers, we can find a thousand and one excuses for anything we dream of doing, but if we are passionate enough about it then we have no excuse at all.

Indeed, where there is a will, there is a way!

Ama xx

3

Don't Worry; God's Got Our Backs

My daughter once brought home a letter from school about an impending school trip. To her, this was a very important field trip and she just could not wait for me to sign and return the letter to school as that would guarantee her attendance. However, to her dismay the next morning, her precious letter was nowhere to be found. She searched everywhere possible asking me umpteen times when and where I had last seen it. I assured her that she should not worry because the school could easily give me another copy to sign. She said OK, but I could tell she was still worried. She kept looking for it till we left the house.

I laughed to myself as I watched her because she was still worried in spite of the fact that we already had a solution to the problem. Then, it hit me: that is probably how God feels when we, His children, worry about challenges He already has the answers to! For some time now, I have been worrying. Actually, if I'm being honest, for the longest time now I have been worrying about everything: from the dangers of this world to the uncertainties of the future and everything negative in between them. Time and again, I would read a Scripture or two in the Bible in which God would tell me not to worry and I would say, "OK Daddy, I totally trust You because You've always been there for me." Sadly, in spite of this affirmation I sometimes forget and go back to worrying.

Why do I feel the need to share this? Well, I know that I am not the only one who worries and if you are a mother like me, then you totally know what I am going on about. But just as I need to remind myself that God knows much more than I do and He will help me, I would like to encourage you to also stop worrying because He really has got our backs. These days I ask myself; "Is it possible that I love myself and the people I care about more than how God loves us all?" Obviously not! So why the worrying?

This year is pregnant with possibilities not uncertainties. Always remember that God has got your back no matter the situation. You are a child of the Creator of this limitless universe; He already has the answers to the questions you are yet to ask. Really, seek Him first and ALL other things will be added to you. Stop worrying and swag your fabulous self!

Ama xx

4
That Annoying Tinge Of Jealousy

I was once among a group of women who had the privilege of chatting with the Managing Director of a leading bank in Ghana and one of his executives. As usual, I was very excited, telling them about the mission of my organisation, The Fabulous Woman Network, which is to celebrate, develop and inspire women to shine in their own corners.

This was me: "We are a network of women who believe in inspiring each other to achieve our potential. We do not agree with the assertion that 'women are their own worst enemies'. We support each other." Blah, blah, blah... Suddenly, the other executive interrupted with "Don't you ever get jealous of each other?" Without even blinking, I responded, "Of course, it is quite possible that you may experience at least a tinge of jealousy when you see what others have achieved. But predominantly when we see others succeed, we are inspired by their success and are encouraged by the knowledge that if our sisters can succeed, then so can we." I blurted out this response without thinking but as I thought about it later, I realised it was the truth, a truth I had come by through experience.

A few years back, I used to look at my friends, who were

doing very well in my opinion, and felt sad because I thought I had not accomplished much. For instance, while I was at my last job, I met a university mate who had a job that was to-die-for (in my opinion, Hahahaha!). She worked at a prestigious law firm while studying law. When I inquired about the nature of her work, she told me how she had to travel a lot, especially to The Hague and London. Of course, she told me it was not all rosy as there were times she cried herself to sleep when her boss made her life miserable. I remember thinking, "Well, I also have a boss who makes me miserable; it would be nice if I could compensate that with trips to London and The Hague!"

Did I feel a tinge of jealousy? Yes! Here I was, giving birth and growing fat while my friends got their masters and law degrees and saved the world. Looking back, I realise the clue I missed was to channel that jealousy into positive energy that would inspire me to do something about my situation if I didn't like it. Let me explain it this way: as I type this piece, this same friend, who has now been called to the bar, is on an amazing trip with other accomplished women carefully selected by a top women's advocate Non-Governmental Organisation to be trained and nurtured for executive positions. Now, this is to absolutely die for! But this time, instead of feeling that annoying tinge of jealousy, I am super-excited for her. I look at her and think: if she can go there, I can also go places! I am so inspired by her achievement that just writing this makes me smile (Hahahaha, I just caught myself grinning!).

The fact is that there will always be those moments when you see others going further in life. That is OK. To each, her own race. I have developed a strategy: whenever good old Miss Tinge of Jealousy sets in, I lead my mind into believing that if another can achieve success, so can I. This 'trick' gives me the energy that I need to push myself and it is now very important for me to see other fabulous women succeeding. Interestingly now that I crave to see successful women, I see them all around me. One minute a friend is being named a brand ambassador, another minute another friend has started her second dream business. I tell you, success is literally sprawling all around me, and this excites me!

The clear message this sends me is that my own success is on its way. These women whom my organisation celebrates did not become successful overnight. While I slept, they prayed. While I took a little slumber, they worked. While I complained, they trudged on. Now, they are relentless, resilient, positive, smart, and fabulous. They have been there, done that. Now, they slay! I bet that the mistakes I recall with dread; they have made even more of those in order to get to where they are today. So no, I have no right to feel sad or get jealous. Instead, I have the responsibility to cheer them on and a privilege to be inspired by their success.

That Annoying Tinge Of Jealousy

Dear reader, next time you see a friend go higher, applaud her outwardly and tell yourself, "If she has achieved her dream, so can I." Channel that jealousy into an amazing energy that spurs you into new territories. And don't worry about having to share the limelight with anyone because there really is more than enough room in the universe for each one of God's creations to shine. If you don't believe me, take a trip to another city and see the stretch of unadulterated land yearning to be occupied! You are fabulous!

Ama xx

5
Be Careful, But Of Whom?

You know how they say be careful whom you call a friend? Well, I sometimes wonder how to tell who to actually be careful of. I mean, some people should get Nobel awards for excelling in keeping their true feelings about others bottled up for months, years, and sometimes even decades!

For instance, I had a very good female friend a few years back who was almost as close as a sister. She cooked the best banku and okro stew for both of us to eat. We used to spend so much time together that everyone in our neighbourhood knew we were besties. Now there was a guy who had a crush on me (OK fine, I had a crush on him too hahahaha). He became part of my girlish dreams and our giggly conversations. One day, my crush warned me to be careful of my best friend, alleging that she hated me. I thought that was ridiculous. He kept repeating this warning but I couldn't be bothered.

He got so frustrated that he promised to prove that he was telling the truth. Hmmmm! In his hand was a letter written by my bestie to my crush and trust me, it was an eye-opening letter. My bestie had 'dressed' me from head to toe in insults using all sorts of forbidden words, advising him to forget about me and go out with her instead! Boy, was I shocked, and I must say, somewhat amused! This was someone I called my bestie! I decided not to let her know that I knew about her betrayal. Instead somehow, by the grace of God, my family moved to Accra. I have not set eyes on her since then. In this case, it was pretty simple to tell whom to be careful of, assuming my crush was being honest.

As we grow older, the situations become more complex. A few years back, I had a boss whom I sometimes thought was impossible! She wore me out with tasks that would make every colleague of mine hate me. There were times I thought she just enjoyed making my life miserable, you know, like she woke up every morning thinking, "Hey, let's go make Ama miserable today!" A number of people warned me about her, saying I should be careful of her because she was out to destroy me. They added that she was using me because she would never do some of the things she asked me to do, blah blah blah. Little did I know that she thought I had a lot of potential and wanted to push me off my lazy bumbum! In fact, in hindsight I know that this lady was God's gift to me because she toughened me.

Fast forward to present day. I still get people telling me every now and then, "Ama, you need to be careful of this or that person." Well, that's great but how do I know whether it is actually the person cautioning me that I need to be careful of? How do I know the truth? In a world in which people are able to smile at you while cursing you in their minds, how does one know who to trust and who not to? Count yourself lucky, if your 'enemy' does not mince words in letting you know that he/she detests you. But if your 'enemy' is actually your 'friend,' and in some wild cases your 'bestie', 'sibling', ' husband or wife', then God be with you. Have you seen the movie 'Awake'?!

What am I rumbling on about? You may walk on this earth for a hundred years and not know the right person to trust and whom to be careful of. So, fabulous one, please hand those who hate you over to God, OK? Be kind to everyone, whether you know for sure that they are your enemy or friend, not because you crave to be in their good books. Do it for God and watch Him take care of you and your business. If you are sure of who your enemy is, then good for you. Commit him/her to God and be careful. But trust me, there are others you may never know hate you, so instead of being afraid and fretting over who to be careful of, do as Psalm 91:1 says and continue to be your fabulous self!

Ama xx

6
Women Are Our Own Angels

Ever since I joined the Ghanaian corporate world, I have been hearing the phrase: 'Women are their own worst enemies'. I find it quite amusing actually and interestingly, I always hear men say it. Today, I would like to propose that this phrase be revised.

Here's why:

1. Yes, I have personally witnessed women in the workplace who cannot stand to see other women grow and concoct evil plans to get rid of them. I have seen women spread false rumors about innocent people, set traps for them and yet pretend to be friends with them. I have no doubt that these things happen women-to-women. However, I have one question: how do we categorize men who get jealous of their female colleagues' achievements, backbite them, and yet smile and chitchat with them in the corridors? How about men-to-men or women-to-men jealousy, which leads to unspoken feud? Note: in my short corporate experience I have seen quite a number of these. Yet, we tend to make it look as if women are the only gender who sabotage each other.

2. How many of us have not heard inspiring stories about how women are mentoring younger women to be

successful in their careers, businesses, family life, etc.? Personally, I have been inspired and helped by a lot of people, most of whom are women. In fact, this is one of the reasons why I started The Fabulous Woman Network in the first place: so that women who are making a difference in our lives in spite of their own challenges can be celebrated as they should be.

From where I sit, both men and women can, and do, sabotage others so there is no point in making this a 'woman' thing. It is a distracting statement, actually. Here is what I think: if men - our dearest husbands, brothers, uncles, fathers, and male colleagues- insist on making this about women, then the phrase should be: 'WOMEN ARE THEIR OWN ANGELS'. Because there are so many women who are touching and impacting lives in positive ways without being jealous or feeling threatened. I love saying, 'There is more than enough room for us all to shine in this universe,' because I actually believe it. Perhaps I cannot change the entire world, but for the rest of my life, I would love to celebrate women who are angels among us.

My advice to my fellow gender mates: you know we are angels to each other. Please let us show the world that we are FOR each other and not against each other. I love this quote by The Fabulous Leading Lady Boss, Yawa Hansen-Quao, 'Success for another lady does not spell failure for you.' That is a fact!

Women Are Our Own Angels

And to all Fabulous Women reading this today, if you have in your life a woman who cannot stand your achievements and where God is taking you, remember it's her problem not yours. Be your true fabulous self and let no woman or man move you. You already have the best friend you need: Jesus. Keep rocking!

Ama xx

7

3-Square Meals, Snacks And Brazilian Hair

I just had to get this off my chest! Recently, a quite controversial Ghanaian TV/Radio Personality called Counsellor Lutterodt was trending on social media for making his usually outrageous yet entertaining comments. I would like to mention, for the record, that he has a great sense of humour and that I enjoy watching him.

However, there are two statements he made that I believe are misleading especially to women who are yet to be married. The first statement is: "A man who is not ready for marriage is a man who cannot feed himself three times a day plus snack" and the second statement is: "Women should never contribute to the upkeep of the house. If chop money is not enough to buy salt, cook without salt." While many are lambasting him for suggesting women should not marry poor men (as defined by his first statement), I would like to draw attention to his second statement. Perhaps my understanding is wrong but these statements give the impression that he is asserting that married men have the sole responsibility of financing all family-related expenses. This, I believe, is wrong.

I took it upon myself to study Proverbs 31, which

3-Square Meals, Snacks And Brazilian Hair

describes the virtuous woman (the model Christian woman). Among the fascinating descriptions of this woman was my personal 'lotto' number: Proverbs 31:18: "She sees that her trading is profitable, and her lamp does not go out at night" (New International Version). This tells us that we women must bring home an income because as wives, we also have financial responsibilities. And of course we do this in practise, even though some people refuse to acknowledge this, which surprises me.

I recall an incident that occurred while I was shopping one time. I bumped into a male friend. While we were conversing, he complained about how expensive things were and I responded by saying, "It's true oh. Even the prices of diapers have gone up." With a sly look on his face, he replied "Why are you complaining? Is it your money that buys the diapers?" I cannot even begin to describe how annoyed I felt about his statement! The fact that he simply assumed that my husband gave me money for shopping was just too much for me to handle. Thank God I had found Jesus then! Hahahaha!

The incident at the shop is not a one-off one. There are a number of times I have been asked by different people, "You, what do you use your money for?" These comments always leave me thinking, "Are you serious? I have kids and a family!' The statement that breaks the camel's back for me is: "My money is solely mine, while my husband's money is for both of us." Ah! Who made these rules? Who is teaching these things to young women and allowing them to believe that all their financial responsibilities will be over once they find their 'Mister'? I am further saddened by the effect this is having on young men today. Some of them have a fear of marriage because they believe ALL the financial burden will be on them.

But my question is: is this really the reality? Are all women (or most) spending all their incomes doing what they want with no input in their family's expenses while men provide everything from school fees to toilet tissues? Why are we not telling yet-to-marry women the truth about marriage? Why are we allowing them to indulge in the fantasies that their husbands MUST provide everything?

Here is my proposal for the concluding part of his famous quote: "A woman too is not ready to marry unless she can afford on a daily basis: 3 square meals, snacks and her own Brazilian hair!" My fabulous married sisters, please let's tell our unmarried sisters the truth even if others won't. We owe it to them. Thank you.

Ama xx

8
Be Fabulous, Not Judgemental

You know how we sometimes get 'fila' about some men of God? Well, I once heard a rather unpleasant story about a well-known and well-respected man of God who attempted to sleep with a young lady when she went to his office for counselling. According to the young lady, when she refused and threatened to report him, he retorted, "Nobody will believe you; I'm a well-respected man of God."

Now, I have no proof that this is true but ever since then, I have been sceptical about the said man. The rumor has affected my perception of him to the extent that whenever I see his picture, hear his name or his voice, I instantly dismiss him. Well, not too long ago, while I was scrolling through Facebook to get my usual dose of daily inspiration, I came across a positive quote that touched my heart. As soon as I lifted my finger to 'Like' it, I realized the quote was made by this 'Opana'. Guess what the hypocrite in me did! Yes, I scrolled past it! That was when it occurred to me that I was judging this man based on what I heard. "Shame on you, Ama", I thought. So what if it is true? Is he not human? Does the word of God change because it is spoken by a man of God who is supposedly lying?

Isn't it ridiculous that we judge so easily, forgetting that we are all full of flaws? We expect others to be perfect Christians when we ourselves ask for forgiveness everyday because we fall into sin every now and then. We are all saved by grace; no one is perfect! 1 Thessalonians 5:20 "Do not despise inspired messages." It doesn't matter who is sharing the message, if it is from God and is meant to bless you, then receive it. May God have mercy on us and forgive our hypocritical ways. Be fabulous, not judgemental.

Ama xx

9
Stay Quiet And Let God Do The Talking

For some time now, I have been hearing some not-so-good stuff concerning most people's favourite TV Grandpapa, Bill Cosby. I was following with keen interest as people chastised, insulted, booed and ridiculed him. In fact, I also wondered if he actually did what he was being accused of; if it's true then that would be quite sad really.

But today, whether he is guilty or not is not the focus for this blog. My attention was drawn to 'how' he handled the media for so long; his silence. It was amazing! How many people can look on quietly and go about minding their own business when millions of people hate and chastise them? I am trying to recall the times I have thrown dramatic tantrums because someone accused me of saying something I didn't; even thinking about them now makes my blood boil, I tell you! So how on earth did Mr. Cosby manage to stay quiet for so long? It must take a great deal of tough skin to endure that! My!

Is it because he is guilty and has no excuse? Is it because he is not guilty but knows that no matter what he says, the odds are against him? Or is it simply because he does not hear what people are saying? Or perhaps, he hears but simply refuses to react?! Whatever the reason, I am personally awed by his ability to control his emotions in public.

I had been pondering over this for some time. I had also been pondering over the fact that there were some people in my life who could not seem to stand me for some reason. It amazes me though because these are people I really respect but the sort of things they mete out to me are not so pleasant. So one day as I was, you know, getting my worship on, trying to get Him (Papa in Heaven) to explain to me why some people simply hated other people for no reason, a word came to me and I wrote it down immediately (thinking I would use it as a Fabulous Woman quote). Here it is:

Fact: Not everyone will like you, no matter what you do or how nice you are to them.

Question: Why focus on changing to please those who don't like you when changing will only make you miserable?

Lesson: Do yourself a favour and be yourself for God to use you as He created you to be.

With these nuggets of wisdom in mind, I resolved to ensure that when my so-called 'haters' lashed out at me, I would simply ignore them, you know, Bill Cosby style hahahaha. In fact, this was something I had been practicing little by little for some time now but I decided to tighten my belt on that and focus on bettering myself to give off my best to God. You won't believe this, barely two hours after writing this, there was an issue in which I was being accused of wrongdoing (as usual! Hahahaha). I knew in my heart of hearts that I was not guilty but who was I to talk? My accuser was so loud, throwing tantrums and causing people to ask what was wrong. I say it to the glory of God that yours truly, The Fabulous Ama Duncan kept quiet through it all and went about my business Bill Cosby style. It was not until I was called to explain myself that I talked about this issue. And God being so good, I was exonerated. I could have fought back, lashed out, retorted, used abusive words...but on this day, this special day of learning, I went to another level of mastering the art of silence.

Dear Reader, I would like to encourage you today to join me on this journey of learning when to shut up and let God fight on our behalf. Indeed, when you hear stories about the negative things people are saying about you, you know without a doubt that we are not battling flesh and blood. There must be some forces at work. Thank God we have Him to battle for us. It is well, OK? Remember this anonymous quote: Never waste too much time explaining yourself. Your friends don't need it and your enemies won't believe it! Stay quiet and let God do the talking.

Ama xx

10
I Must Mirror My Fabulous Sister

I want to tell you about my friend; we will call her 'Trisha' so she doesn't chew me when she reads this. She is such a lady, always composed no matter the situation. She laughs, sits, walks, stands...does everything just like a lady. As I write this article, she is about six months pregnant and boy, you should see her! Make-up always on point, hair clean, tidy and classy, well-dressed every time, so calm and collected, and she still manages her business, performs her mummy/wife duties. She is really The Fabulous Woman!

However, she has one tiny problem: Trisha does not see just how fabulous she is. No, she doesn't see herself as possessing these great attributes I see in her. In fact, she once told her sister in these exact words, "When Ama Duncan is describing me, it's as if she's talking about someone else." Like seriously? How on earth is Trisha not able to see how fabulous she is? I wonder!

One day, I was talking to my husband about Trisha, going on and on about how I couldn't understand why she just refused to see the beautiful side of her. I was frustrated with her and I wished I could make her see what I saw in her. I was moaning tirelessly when my husband interrupted me with "Oh, you mean she's like you?" That hit me, hard! But of course, I recovered quickly and pretended he hadn't said anything at all while this dearest husband of mine just shook his head, laughed at me and went about his business.

I knew very well that he had spoken the truth: like a lot of fabulous women, I hardly ever see the good in me. I know quite a number of women who feel as Trisha (and I) does- unable to see just how fabulous they are. Sometimes when I contact women I deem inspiring and ask them to share their stories on The Fabulous Woman Network, the typical answer I get is "Hahahaha! Me? My story is still being written. You wait, when I accomplish A, B and C, you can share my story." They leave me thinking, "Oh my God, how can this woman not know how inspirational her story already is?"

Why is it so? Why do we always see other people as all that: perfect, beautiful, confident, fabulous, etc., but never see such in our own selves? We see other people's marriages, jobs, looks and homes as better than ours. Recently, when we were talking about this subject, Trisha said to me, "Maybe God made some of us that way so as to let us remain humble." Perhaps it's true, perhaps it's false.

One thing I know for sure is that I feel good when someone tells me my positives even though my initial reaction is usually to dismiss what they are saying. For this reason, I have decided to make a conscious effort to mirror my fellow fabulous sisters' positives. I will point out the good in them because I know how it feels to be praised: it makes me strive to be better. Even God enjoys praise and requires that from mankind.

Ama Duncan's pledge to Trisha and all my fabulous sisters: I will make a deliberate effort to mirror you. I will drum your positives into your head until you believe them. Will you mirror me too so that we can shine together? I believe that there is enough room in the universe for us ALL to shine as God created us to.

Ama xx

11
Is That A Whole Box Of Prawns?

Sometimes when I recall some of my most embarrassing moments, I burst into laughter. Some of them are just too ridiculous. I shall tell you one of such incidents. My partner and I lived in a little village in the West Midlands of United Kingdom. We had a favourite Chinese restaurant which served amazing prawns! Now, the best part of their buffet service was that they would give you a take-out pack for £5.5; all you had to do was to fill it up with as many items as the pack could contain. I am sure you have guessed by now what yours truly did. My partner and I would cook rice at home and then walk over to our unsuspecting Chinese restaurant, smile nicely at them as we ordered our take-out packs, saunter ever-so-leisurely towards the buffet and pick as many prawns as the poor take out-pack could carry! Before you judge, please let me finish.

One day as we embarked on our usual routine and got to the counter, this obviously-not-amused Chinese waitress who had probably noticed us from day one and could not stand us, looked at our pack and asked (rather meanly, I mean, come on we were still customers. Or?), "Is that a whole box of prawns?" I am sure if I had had any liquid in my bladder, it would have flown out freely! We were so embarrassed by that question but had to put up brave faces. Mercifully, madam detective-waitress' manager saved the day by signalling that she should let us go. Whew! That was too close. My partner and I laughed all the way home and till date, we occasionally recall this incident and laugh.

This was years ago, but today as I remembered this experience, it hit me that we were utterly greedy! I mean, we sometimes literally emptied the chaffing dish of prawns leaving behind rice, noodles, etc. without caring much how other customers would also enjoy their buffet. And I have seen this behaviour one too many times at restaurant buffets across Ghana. When customers are given the opportunity to dish their own food, some of them usually empty dishes of soups, stews, and meat into their own plates. How can we be this greedy? How can we not care that the people who come in later will not have meat, stew or soup at the buffet?

In this country, we love to accuse political leaders of being selfish, nonchalant, greedy, corrupt, and not giving a hoot about the people. Yet, we as individuals forget our own callous actions and we fail to see the impact of the choices we make on later generations. We just do what we want to do now and move on; we are not bothered about how this affects others. We throw rubbish beside bins even when the bin is wide open. We throw rubbish on the streets from inside the trotro. We choke our gutters with so much waste and move on unconcerned. After all, we don't live in that neighbourhood, so how can flooding in that area possibly be our headache right? Wrong!

You know the people who get caught up in the floods, well they are human beings like us too. They most likely work very hard to contribute to our economy just like us. They have children, parents, boyfriends and girlfriends, are bread winners, just like us. They have dreams and aspirations of owning their own multi-million dollar companies, just like us. Wouldn't it be really cool if we could take a moment to think about the effect our actions have on others before we actually act? Wouldn't it be really fabulous if we could care enough about the next customer coming to buy fufu and leave some of the goat meat in the light soup for them? I think such little individual acts will do wonders for Ghana our beloved country.

If we want our leaders to care, then we must show care. If we want them to stop being greedy, then let us stop being greedy. Because you know what, leadership starts with us. Leaders are made or chosen from amongst us; they are not heavenly creatures. If we cannot care for one another now, how can we care about the citizens when we become leaders?

So my friend reading this today, the next time you are at a buffet about to scoop all the prawns, goat meat, cake, chicken or whatever it is that makes your mouth water, stop and think: what will the next person have if I finish everything? The next time you leave rubbish in any place but a bin, ask yourself: would I want my room to look like this? Hopefully, you wouldn't. I wouldn't either, and so I pledge to make an intentional effort to avoid greed, going forward. So help me God.

Ama xx

12
My Boots, My Right

I love boots, and though I own only two pairs (to my shame hahahaha), I wear them as often as possible. Thus, during a recent event my team organized, I decided to wear my favourite pair. I planned way ahead what I would wear and how I would look. As the day drew closer, I realized that the clothes might not look as perfect as I had pictured they would look, but aaahhh, I still had my favourite boots so I knew I would feel good on the D-day.

The big day arrived, and yes, I wore my boots! Oh yes! I felt really good in them! To me, everything about my look was perfect! I was wearing my boots, wasn't I? And oh, the icing on the cake was when the really nice Master of Ceremony commented that my boots 'were on fleek!' Imagine my excitement! To add a perfect finish, a couple of people sent me messages about my boots after the event! My day was officially perfect with that comment!

But! Apparently, a few friends thought the boots were a no-no! "Boots during a daytime event? No, Ama! We don't do that!" they lamented. Really? I had no idea that I was breaking a code! My friends had a field day teasing me, a couple of weeks later when they brought it up. I was actually quite surprised because I had never looked at it from their perspective.

My Boots, My Right

Will I wear boots again for a daytime event? Absolutely! Hahahaha! Why? Because life is too short! You see, I have learnt that there are so many things we may love to do as human beings but cannot do because they may hurt other people or breed envy. Like when I eat my brother's jollof because it looks so delicious even though I know he is super hungry: that hurts him. Or when I covet my sister's brand new 'tear rubber' Chrysler and wish it will get a scratch: that is envy. However, as for my boots they do not hurt anyone, oh and hopefully do not breed any envy. In fact, in hindsight they performed a very important function on that day.

1. I felt really good in them!

2. Those who loved it, smiled!

3. Those who thought it was a no-no, laughed!

So in the end, it was a win-win for all of us. Tell me, why won't I wear my boots again for a daytime event? Essentially, I am saying that: not everything is permissible, I admit. But for the few one or two harm-free things we can do to feel good, have a good laugh and create priceless memories from, we must actually do them because really life is not that long. What if ghosts don't get to wear boots? Eh? We must live!

Ama xx

13
Order From Above: Be Submissive

Recently, I had an opportunity to sit with an old friend whom I had not seen for ages. We blabbed a lot about everything! In ten minutes, we tried to get a quick update on everything that had gone on in our lives over all these years we had been apart- you know us ladies *wink*. My friend had a very successful career as a lawyer and was doing big things; I was very happy for her. But of course, my konkonsa self would not let her go without asking her if she was dating anyone special. To my utter surprise, she told me that most of the men in her life were intimidated by her career success and usually backed off! Yes, I was surprised because I had indeed heard of such stories but I never actually thought in practice men were intimidated by successful women.

Not only was this fabulous woman Fanti, she also was very beautiful in all the right places, smart and God-fearing. Which man would not want to take her home to meet his Mama? We both agreed that if we were men, we would love for our wives to be successful so that we could feel proud and brag to others about them. Later, as I pondered over this issue, I realized that 'No, we are not men and we probably have no right to assume we would have treated women differently'. I wondered, perhaps men were intimidated by successful women because of how they (successful women) have acted in the past.

I cannot believe I am actually admitting this today but yes, SOMETIMES we women disrespect our husbands when we earn as much as or more than them. In such cases, we do not regard them as the head of the home and refuse to submit to them. In fact, sometimes we yell at them as if they are our kids. And yes, we make their lives miserable by flaunting our successes in their faces and making them feel inadequate as men. Some of us consistently spend most of our time trying to make more money and neglect the needs of our men. There is nothing fabulous about that!

So why won't some men refuse to date and marry their co-equals based on these things that we sometimes do? A man will always be a man. Whether we like it or yes! God, in His infinite wisdom, chose the husband to be the head of the home and not the wife. We women must respect this no matter how successful we are. We must still serve our husbands their meals as if they are kings, we must use 'please' when requesting something from them and say 'thank you' when they do something for us. And yes, we MUST say 'sorry' when we are wrong. In fact, a wise fabulous woman says sorry even when she knows she is right because she is smart enough to know that a man has an ego and there is not much she can do about that except pray for patience to deal with it.

Yarns Of Inspiration I

I once heard the story of a woman who was richer than her husband. She wanted to buy a 'tear rubber' car with her own hard-earned money but her husband said no. This woman insisted and bought it anyway. You can imagine the 3rd world war at her home! There is a reason why the Bible commands us to submit to our husbands. A smart woman knows that she wins her husband's love when she is submissive.

Fabulous married woman, you may be the boss at work but the minute you walk through your gates into your home, you are a wife. Don't get me wrong, I don't practice submission to perfection; IT IS HARD! But, let's take it one little step at a time. Make conscious little efforts and gradually we will master the art of submission and hopefully one at a time, more men will see that it really is cool to marry a successful woman. May God help us to be fabulously submissive!

Ama xx

14
Simple, Fabulous And Romantic

I heard the most beautiful story recently about this couple whom I deemed to be pretty romantic in their relationship. They have a great intimate relationship in which the husband actually calls in to check on her quite often during the day; they go for vacations at least twice a year as a priority, the wife cooks all these exotic dishes for him regularly, I mean they are really nice to each other. One tradition they hold dearly is exchange of presents (usually expensive gifts) during anniversaries which they practice religiously for birthdays, wedding anniversaries, mother's or father's day among others.

In a conversation with my friend (the woman) and in my usual hopelessly romantic mode, I asked her what she got this year for their wedding anniversary, expecting something like a surprise trip to Sao Tome. Instead, she said she got a letter from him! I tell you, my smile was as wide as the Atlantic Ocean when she told me the content of the letter. To sum it up, he thanked her for sticking with him through the hard times, assuring her of his continuous love and promising her he will make it up to her in future. My friend told me, 'His words felt like diamonds to me!' In fact, of all the romantic things I have seen this man do to woo his wife, this certainly tops them all: a simple letter to his beloved assuring her of his undying love and appreciation for her. In my mind, I had crowned him one of the most romantic men on earth for this alone.

I wonder why sometimes we refuse to be romantic with excuses such as 'I don't have money', 'the time is not right' or 'I am too busy'. Some of the most romantic stories I have heard involved no money, just creativity, thoughtfulness and good old sweetness.

So couples, next time you are planning a romantic do for your sweetheart, don't worry too much if the times are hard in your pocket. Just be creative, thoughtful and sweet in your delivery because the effect will be fabulous!

Ama xx

15
The Dreadful Road To Bravery

I once read somewhere that one of the commonest fears among human beings is the fear of speaking in public? Really? For me, that is usually not a problem at all. I mean, I stand before people lots of times as part of my work. However, I battle with another fear (well lots, but I shall write about only one for now...HEIGHT!). Let me tell you a story...

Once upon a time, probably 20 years ago, I promised myself NEVER EVER to go on the Kakum National Park (Cape Coast, Ghana) canopy walkway again! All I can recall from the trip was that it was super scary and I did number one (yes! Wee-weed!) three times on the seven-course canopy walkway. You see, I have a deep fear of heights. As for flying on a small plane, it kills me. From the minute I know I have to fly between Kumasi-Accra, I will fret and fret until on the D-day when the plane actually lands and I promise myself NEVER to fly again.

Back when I was in Archbishop Porter Girls' Secondary School (Takoradi, Ghana), I managed to say no to the canopy walkway although most of my mates went on it during a class trip. I had resolved not to do it and nothing was ever going to change that. Well, until recently when my family took a trip to the coast again. Hmmm, we decided to go to Kakum but of course I knew I was not going on the canopy walkway so I was not perturbed. However, after the Receptionist cajoled my kids to go along, I said to myself, 'Courage is not the absence of fear...I will talk to my mind the same way I talk to it whenever I am on a flight'. Then, I said to my husband, 'I must not deny the kids this adventure just because of my fear of heights.' We reached a decision: we were all going!

We got to the edge, I took one look at it and every molecule in me screamed 'No!' Yet I was not ready to give up this time. I went anyway, my husband ahead, followed by our son, our daughter and then me. Surprisingly, the kids were not that scared, perhaps because we were with them or they simply did not understand what all the fuss was about. But as for me, I was literally melting, I felt this strange surge of unexplainable lightness in my chest. About five steps in, as the dreadful canopy creaked, rose and fell, I started repeating, 'We can do this, don't look down, just keep your eye on Daddy's big head.' I must have said it about a hundred times during the first course alone and it got the kids giggling. I also feigned some giggles. Fact was, I was saying it more to myself than to them. I was so terrified, I refused to look down but kept looking at my husband's head and kept talking to distract myself from my fear.

I would have loved to tell you that I finished the full seven-course walkway, but I could not. I simply did not have the heart to go through with it. Although I kept talking and saying positive things for courses two and three, I took the shortcut after the second course. Lessons learnt?

1. It is better to start something and fail than not to start at all. Oh, the feeling when I finished the three-course...priceless!

2. Always, ALWAYS stay focused on a positive thing. The environment may look scary but pick a focus and keep your eye there until your goal is achieved. Trust me, if I had taken my eye off my husband's head, I would have most likely laid flat on the canopy walkway, refusing to move until I was drugged into an artificial coma and rescued!

3. Finally, we all as individuals battle different kinds of fears, hence we must not impose our fears on our kids. Had we not taken our kids along, we would not have known that they could go on the walkway without any fears. In fact, they actually want to go back! These kids! Lord help me!

As I continue on my journey to build a global brand for women empowerment, I face all sorts of hurdles: uncertainties, self-doubt, fear of failure, fear of being laughed at, etc., but the vision on my heart is too fabulous not to come to fruition. I will press on, repeating positive mantras to myself, keeping my eye on that vision and my mind on my Father in Heaven. As for the Kakum Canopy

Walkway, I will go back to finish it another time and when I do, I will know that I have finally graduated from the Pre-school of Bravery. I will overcome!

Ama xx

16
The Table Or The Enemy?

In February 2016, I had the opportunity to lead my team to organize our first conference for women in Kumasi, Ghana. Like every event, we had our own challenges with venue, marketing, sponsorship...the usual. But one personal challenge I battled with before, during and even after the event was: my 'enemies'. Of course, I'm not the most-liked or nicest person on earth, so obviously I am very much aware that not everyone smiling with me and patting my back wants me to succeed. In fact, there were certain people that I was absolutely sure were looking forward to the event being a total flop. Interestingly, each time I worried about how people would laugh if the event was unsuccessful, a Bible text came to mind: You set a table before me in the presence of my enemies. (Psalm 23:5). In spite of this reassurance, my stubborn head would still worry occasionally.

A day before the event, someone made a comment about how I should not worry about getting a big venue because not that many people were coming anyway. I was not happy with the comment but I told God about it and reminded Him that this event was for Him. Mind you, although we had planned to have two hundred people from the start, we ordered three hundred chairs and

The Table or The Enemy?

snacks...Big faith right?

Well, the day of the event arrived. So far so good, things were on course. About an hour into the conference I looked at the half-empty room and asked God in my head "Daddy, so are you going to allow my 'enemy' to laugh at me and say 'I told you so?'" I also reminded Him of my earlier prayer that everyone who came for the event would be touched and inspired to shine some more. After this short prayer, I went about my duties making sure everything was on course. Long story short, in the end we had three hundred plus participants at The Fabulous Woman Speaks '16. Oh, but that was not even the most exciting part, it was the countless positive feedback we had afterwards. I was actually in awe!

Later, as I sat down quietly to let Daddy upstairs know how grateful I was for giving us success and that He did not allow me to be embarrassed, the same scripture came to mind again: 'You set a table before me in the presence of my enemies'. This really got me thinking. Wait a minute, if God has promised to set a table before me in the presence of my enemies, why on earth is my focus on the 'enemy' and not the 'table'? Why have I spent precious time thinking about how much some people would have rejoiced had the program been a flop? When did their business become my headache anyway? In fact, I felt ashamed as I realized how ridiculous I had been. Forgive me Daddy, I need to work on my faith!

Child of God, whether we like it or not, His promise to us stands: He will set a table before us in the presence of our enemies. Ours is to focus on the fabulous dishes displayed before us and enjoy them to His delight. We will not acknowledge our enemies not because we are ignorant of their existence, but because we remember His other promise that our enemy will be His enemy. From this day, I will endeavor to focus on the table before me. Will you? Enjoy your meal!

Ama xx

17
Young Fabulous Woman, Wake Up And Make Your Dream A Reality!

When I was little, I was a dreamer. I would sit for hours fantasizing about a totally different life in which I was rich, attended a rich British boarding school, met Prince William and lived happily ever after. I would watch Telenovelas and lust after the lavish lifestyle of the rich ladies in their stilettos, plush homes and fancy convertible cars. And I was hopeful that one day, my fantasies would become reality. After all, if people could win the lottery or suddenly inherit some mega money, why couldn't the Prince fall in love with a small-town Komenda (Ghana) girl like me?

Well, of all the ways through which I fantasized my wealth, I do not recall hard work as one of the options. On and on I hoped and fantasized that someday my dreams would come true. It was not until I lived alone in England where I had to pay my own bills through 'sweat in chills,' that it dawned on me that no manna was going to drop from heaven, and that I had to work hard and smart to enjoy the things I fantasized about - at least the material ones because as for meeting Prince William, it was going to take a gargantuan miracle! Hahahaha

Sadly, I realize that a lot of us young ladies continue to fantasize about glamorous lives but are not ready to earn it. While some of us are praying day and night for money to fall from the skies into our bank accounts, others are chasing after rich pot-bellied men to cater to our needs and wants. We have no idea what rich people have to do to make money. While we sleep, they are up working and strategizing. While we are moaning about how hard things are these days, they are devising innovative ways to increase their productivity.

A number of rich people, including a few I know, started off by doing manual jobs like cleaning gutters, washing dirty dishes at hotels, selling 'pure water', etc. Surprisingly, I find that some of us who desire to be rich, are not prepared to start from scratch. Some of us will never be caught dead sweeping or selling from head pans but what we fail to realize is that there is a lot to learn from such jobs if we want to be rich too. We want to finish school and immamediately land that dream job that pays us dollars, gives us a company car and an apartment, plus vacation allowance for trips abroad.

We see rich people and covet their lives. We spend all day on the couch watching 'Keeping up with the Kardashians' and expect that our lives will dramatically transform into theirs. Young Fabulous Woman, if you dream of a certain lifestyle, be prepared to earn it. Isn't it refreshing to see an industrious, financially-independent, fabulous woman who can stand on her own two feet? Stop fantasizing and make your dream a reality because in you is fabulous!

Ama xx

18
The Mandela Way

Nelson 'Madiba' Mandela. I, like many people around the world, salute this legend. I have heard stories about him that make him seem unreal. First of all, the man spent twenty-seven years in jail, never gave up his dream but instead fought through thick and thin to liberate his country from apartheid. Then he managed to get out of jail and subsequently, became the first black president of the country. What I found most surprising about him was his intentional effort to forgive those who put him in jail. I see this as his most powerful attribute. It is actually on record that he invited three of his former jailers (who were nice to him) into his home to dine with him and his guests after his inauguration as president. Wow!

Thinking about him and forgiveness, I am forced to take a look at my own life and how at one point or the other, I have been hurt by people I thought I could trust. To forgive them is not easy at all. Actually, let me confess that sometimes it feels good to muse over their actions because then I get to think of all the God-forsaken words I would rain on them should I be given the opportunity. Some of these words I probably will never dare utter, but at least the thought gives me some kind of relief. But does it really? I know for a fact, that holding on to the thought of someone else's negative actions cause me unbearable pain. Sometimes I actually lose sleep and end up unable to focus on anything productive. And, the number of times I sigh is just ridiculous! Un-forgiveness cripples me! What if we flipped the coin? What about all the people I have hurt deeply, some of whom I may not even be aware of? Do they also enjoy musing over my actions, and address me with all sorts of words in their heads? If they do, I may never know.

This one thing I know for sure: 'un-forgiveness' hurts the 'un-forgiver' more than the 'un-forgiven'. It is ironic, isn't it? Because when we refuse to forgive others, we are actually trying to 'punish' them, right? Wrong. I have recently come to realize that Mandela was right when he said, 'As I walked out the door toward the gate that would lead to my freedom, I knew if I didn't leave my bitterness and hatred behind, I'd still be in prison'. This is a simple truth shared by a man of great wisdom.

The Christians among us celebrate Easter, a season in which the most remarkable show of love and forgiveness occurred with the death of our Jesus Christ. During this season and at all times, I pray that we learn to love ourselves enough to forgive others as Christ forgave us, because at the end of the day forgiving others is really in our best interest. A thought: if we find it too difficult to forgive others, let's flip the coin and remember the times we have been forgiven for our own mistakes.

If we want to move forward as a nation, then we must really let go of the pain of the past by making an intentional effort to let go of it. The bitterness, the anger, the long hours of musing and sighing, the plotting to pay people back with their own coins are all not worth our time and effort. As a people, we need to go the Mandela way in order to be free to make history.

Ama xx

19

When Jesus Says Yes...

While I was dancing to Michelle Williams' song "When Jesus says Yes, Nobody can say No" and totally enjoying the words and tempo because they resonated exactly how I felt, a friend came into my office and saw me dancing.

Friend: You know a friend of mine says that song is a Satanist song?

Me (surprised): Really? Why?

Friend: Well, she gave a long list of reasons why...

Me: Well that's her opinion. We all have our opinions.

After he left, I started to wonder why such a song would be labeled 'Satanist'. I mean, the lyrics talk about Jesus and I know Michelle Williams is a Gospel Singer. I must confess though that in the video I saw sister Beyoncé looking lovely in a nice dress with side slits, which showed off her hot pants underneath the dress. I thought, 'That's so Beyoncé!' I began to wonder what God thought of that but didn't really take the time to think about it much as I was enjoying the song.

However, later my friend's comment came back to haunt me. What makes a song a 'gospel' one? Is it the words?

The personality who wrote/sang it? The spirit backing it? If it is about the words, then it is definitely easier to identify. But if it is about the personality or spirit behind the song, then we are in deep Barney rubble. How does one actually KNOW another person? Her heart, her thoughts, and the spirit she consults in the secret of her mind? And what about the person who does not know the songwriter/singer at all but hears the song and is moved to praise His God?

Really, I think as children of God, we are sometimes too hard on ourselves, judging every little detail of everyone else's actions while we overlook our own impure ways. At the end of the day, when we stand before God to be judged, it will be between Him and the individual: 'me'. For instance, there will be no room for, 'Oh and, God did You notice what Beyoncé was wearing in that video? *Shaking my head* Bad, bad Beyoncé!' It will only be about the individual and her actions or inactions. It will be very interesting to see the persons we perceived to be ungodly, opening Heaven's gates and sitting at the right hand of God when we get to heaven. What did God say about our righteousness again? It is as filthy rugs! Yes! Ours is not to judge who is right or wrong. Our responsibility is to have a rich personal relationship with Him so that He can use us for His glory while we are here on earth. This business of labeling anyone who doesn't behave like we do as ungodly is a bit suffocating actually. OK bye bye, I'm off to dance! When Jesus says yes,

When Jesus Says Yes...

nobody can say no...!

Ama xx

20
Fabulous Woman, It's OK To Make The First Move!

Have you ever had a crush? You know, that feeling you have when you see someone you really like and your heart misses a beat? When you as much as sense his cologne, all of a sudden you can't think of anything else but him? You gape at him so much that you run into a wall and bump your head? I bet you have had your share of this utterly confusing yet miserably beautiful feeling or whatever it is that is referred to as a crush.

Let me tell you about one of my crushes from when I was an innocent little University of Ghana, Legon girl. For privacy purposes, let's call him Teddy, shall we? Oh, he was tall and lanky! Friends who were close to me then knew these two descriptions totally drove me crazy but if he played any musical instrument at all, well then, of course, I would simply be 'drunk in crush'. Hmmm, Teddy was actually a good friend, or more accurately a bit more of a 'spiritus' brother to me. We would hang out and talk for hours on end because we had a lot in common.

I remember making pancakes one time and packing them ever-so sweetly into a take-away pack for my Teddy. I walked all the way from my hall to his, wondering if he would like my pancakes. I was quite nervous but I wasn't about to back out now. I told myself that "Vim dey!!!"

Hmmm, and "vim dey-ed" until I got outside his room and peeped through his window only to find my crush, Teddy, chatting with some other 'spiritus' sister in his musical voice. Eiiii!!! This boy kill me oh!! Upon seeing them, I backed away slowly like Jerry who had seen sleeping Tom and did not want any wahala. To be honest, my heart was broken. That night I cried myself to sleep. The next time I saw Teddy, I smiled sweetly at him as if nothing had ever happened and everything went back to normal, except my heart.

I never ever had the courage to let Teddy know I had a crush on him. I was chicken! But actually come to think of it, is this not so because as young ladies we are somehow conditioned to believe that a girl must never make the first move? Recently, I had yet another opportunity to be a panelist on David Akuetteh's Diary Show on Luv FM (Kumasi, Ghana) to discuss the subject of women proposing to men first. My opinion was simple: in your twenties, the idea of being chased is actually exciting! You know, saying no to the poor boy countless times when you're actually nuts over him, until another girl starts getting his attention? That's fun and all. But when you're in your thirties, you most likely know what you want in life and do not have the time or energy to do "No-no-no-yes-no-yes-no-yes-OK-yes-please don't go." At this point, when you have a crush and the person has the potential to be Mr. Right, I don't believe you should lose guard kroaaa. Of course if he is not your friend already, then you

MUST do a background check to ensure he is a correct dude. The check should cover information about his family, workplace, friends, and other important details before you make any moves.

Here is what I propose:

Stage 1: Drop hints: compliment him, be extra attentive, call to check up on him every now and then, invite him over for dinner, go watch a movie, etc. But ladies, we all know sometimes men are either simply clueless or wearing P.O.P., and can simply not make the first move even if their lives depend on it! If this is your wahala, then Fabulous sister, move to:

Stage 2: Be bold and tell him how you feel about him. Look, some men actually find it sexy when the woman makes the first move and I know some of such men. In fact, when I asked a male friend how he would feel if a woman proposed to him first, this was his response: "Me do no rough (I will like her deeply). It's a turn on and I will respect her because it is a sign of confidence." Interestingly, the response from the female callers on the show was 50-50, while ALL the male callers said they would not mind at all if a woman proposes first and they would not respect that woman any less. Well, there you go! It's really in our heads: this fear of being rejected.

A fabulous woman must learn to be bold. Please, don't be a chicken like Ama Mbir (my maiden name), the little

Legon girl! Life is too short for you to die inside anytime you see him but can't hold his hand or hear him say 'I love you'. Love really is beautiful but you need courage to start and sustain it. I say, go for it! Seriously, what have you got to lose? You're already fabulous and nothing can change that!

Ama xx

21
Think. Pray. Eat Jollof And Move!

"Ama, I need your help! I need to move out of my current job. It doesn't even matter if I am paid half of what I earn currently. I just need enough to get by, my family and I will be fine. And most importantly, I will get to spend more time with my family. Ama, you need to help me!" This was a distress call I recently received from a friend. He went on and on trying to let me understand why he needed to leave his current company. I told him, "Don't worry, I understand you perfectly." Coincidentally, this call came at a time when I was preparing to give my first-ever TEDx talk (TEDxAdum) on 'The Quest to Escape My Corporate Trap'. What my friend did not know was that I had also quit my job but for a different reason.

Have you ever been caught in a trap so tight, you wanted to wiggle out but couldn't? I would like to tell you how I was able to get out of my corporate trap, with the hope that this story will inspire you to free yourself from whatever kind of trap you find yourself in. If anyone had told me a year ago, that I would quit my job and focus on my own business full-time, I would have laughed! You see, one of my biggest fears, is the fear of being completely flat-bottom broke. And for this reason, I have worked since I was in the university because for me, working has been the only way to make money. I had a decent monthly income, which was extremely important even though it was never enough for me. I loved the security it gave me because no matter what, I knew I would get paid at the end of the month.

I was employed by a four-star hotel as a Learning and Development Manager. Apart from my salary, I had some really nice pecks like medical insurance for my family and free lunch. It was a respectable position and I got to network with some of the industry's top bosses. As is normal practise for most organisations, our salaries were reviewed at the beginning of each year and I was very much aware that that year's (2016) increment was going to be extraordinary. In fact, it was actually increased by over 50%; but by then I had already resigned.

I am sure you are asking yourself, what was I thinking?! Why on earth did I quit just when my job was about to get sweeter? The answer is simple: I felt it was time and it was the right thing to do. You see, I had been at my job for eight years. Initially, it was an amazing and challenging experience; there was something new to learn every day. I even had the opportunity to lead my department for a couple of years. However after four years, I could literally close my eyes and do my job. The organisation was still a great place to work at, with really nice people who had become like family to me. But clearly, I had become too comfortable and had very little challenge. I knew it was time to move.

Think. Pray. Eat Jollof And Move!

As I prepared to quit my job, I thought about my options: to search for a new job or to start my own business? While the former was not too appealing to me, the latter was an occasional fantasy. I would sometimes imagine what it would be like to run my organisation but I never had a clear picture of what I would be doing. Every time the idea of running my own business came up, I would simply dismiss it, unwilling to explore it further. The fact was, I was terrified! I had never run a serious business before, what if it failed and I actually became completely flat-bottom broke?! I still had financial responsibilities at home! Surely, I couldn't be that selfish and risk everything to pursue a dream that was not even clear! Besides, what was I good at anyway? Who would consult me to do anything for them? I allowed fear and self-doubt to stop me from even considering self-employment, let alone entrepreneurship. Instead I enrolled in a Master's in Business Administration (MBA) course. That MBA was my excuse to say to people who cared enough to ask why I was marking time: "Oh you know I am currently doing an MBA, it is stressful enough combining that with my life as a young mother."

Well, after two years I was done with the MBA. I had my second degree, now what? I still had not figured out my next move even though I had a burning desire to move out of my comfort zone. Interestingly, requests for my professional help intensified as I networked with more people who found out that I was a Corporate Trainer. I would occasionally get invitations to speak to different groups on customer service, personal branding, etc. This was when it finally dawned on me that I had a business opportunity! I say "finally" because a number of very important people in my life, including my husband, had suggested this to me but I always dismissed it.

In 2015, I registered my first business called Corporate Training Solutions with the primary objective of helping our clients increase their productivity through our training and development activities. I was still working full-time then and so I could not take on some contracts due to conflict of interest. There were good businesses that I had to pass on to other consultants because I was unable to handle them. Also, I didn't take the idea of growing my own business to the point of being completely financially-independent seriously. However, the urge to quit my job continued to grow stronger by the day and yet I was not sure what I was going to do next.

During that period, I got wind of a job offer so I decided to give it a shot. I knew from day one that I could not take the job offer for personal reasons but I convinced myself that I needed to sit on the other side of an interview session for a change. I needed the experience of being interviewed just in case I had to actively start looking for a new job. The interview went so well that we ended up chatting. Now, as I look back, I wonder if my confidence was due to the fact that I did not really want the job and was only there out of curiosity. In the end, I was offered the job but I had to turn it down.

In 2015, I founded The Fabulous Woman Network. This literally jolted me back to life! I was so consumed with writing about women, interviewing women, and organising activities to celebrate, develop and inspire women everywhere. That was all I could think of. I was suddenly alive again, happy! One time someone asked me, "Ama, do you get paid for the work you do for The Fabulous Woman Network?" With a smile, I responded 'No'. She shook her head and gave up on me! I was so passionate about celebrating, developing and inspiring women through our activities that I did not even care if I wasn't getting paid for it! By then, I was still hanging on to my full-time job. It was not demanding, but it deserved my attention as I was being paid and frankly, I could not continue with it. Because my zeal had died, I knew my work was done and it was definitely time to move on. However, there was one burning question: how was I going to make money after I had quit my job? Remember, I had always needed the security of being paid at the end of every month. In fact, the more I thought of the idea of quitting my job, the more I asked myself "Ama, are you OK? Why in the world would you risk everything you have for something you do not even know is there?"

Obviously, the money I was making from corporate training was not enough because I never advertised. I realised that I needed help otherwise I was going to dilly-dally forever and keep postponing my final date of resignation. Here is what I did: I spoke to a few people I knew who had 'been there, and had done that.' They all gave very helpful advice on the various options I had at my disposal. One of them, Yawa Hansen-Quao, is actually a Business Coach. She asked me, "What is your monetisation plan?" I had none, even though I needed one badly. She gave me an assignment to come up with a strategy. Yawa was really helpful in that she introduced me to some amazing networks as well as guide me through drafting a winning strategy. I scribbled my first draft down and asked God to give me a sign before I did anything. I was really desperate with a burning desire to quit my job. I needed to be absolutely sure that God was the one asking me to leave, because as a child of God I know with Him in my boat, I will smile through the rain, the sunshine and the storm.

One day, I followed my husband on a trip so that while he was in meetings, I could spend time alone to pray and think, away from my children. I prayed, I thought and oh, I ate jollof! Hahahaha! By evening, I had made my decision and finalized my strategy. I had a discussion with my husband when he returned, and I was fortunate to have his support (Bless him!).

When I returned to work, I finally did the right thing; I tendered in my resignation. Trust me, it felt so good! To make things a bit more interesting, two days before my last day of work as I was getting ready to hand over, I received a call from an unknown number. In fact, I wanted to ignore the call but I realised that same number had called my other mobile line earlier. I thought, "This must be important." Apparently, the caller was the Human Resource Director of a five-star hotel, an international brand. She informed me about a vacancy which was literally to-die-for and asked if I was interested. What you would have done, if this were you? Well, I humbly declined because I finally knew what I needed to do and getting another job was not going to help my strategy at this time. You see, I needed freedom to control what I did with my time. I needed to be able to move around to market my brand on and off air. I needed to be available to attend some of the exciting events home and away. Working for someone else 8 a.m. 5 p.m. everyday gave me very little extra time to do these. I could not leave one job just to jump into another even if the salary was way more than I was getting at my old job.

One of the most important parts of my strategy is continuous personal development. Like I said, I have never run a serious business before unless selling cocoa drink and tangerine when I was a child counts! Thus, I am always on the lookout for opportunities to learn. If there is a seminar on entrepreneurship or leadership, count me in! If there is a book, please I want it! In fact, a friend was kind enough to send me an amazing book, "The E-Myth Revisited" by Michael E. Gerber. Another fabulous sister-from-another-mother, Rosalin Abigail Kyere-Nartey also told me about the YALI (Young African Leaders Initiative) leadership course. I quickly applied and got accepted.

The experience I had? Well, I will share it another time. But I can tell you this for now, it was definitely worth the five weeks away from my family.

To the glory of God, now I have two businesses (and one quiet one). Corporate Training Solutions focuses on helping organisations improve their productivity by training and developing their employees. My team and I have trained over six hundred participants (as of December, 2016) from various organisations on customer service skills. This is where we make money to put food on the table as well as fund the activities of The Fabulous Woman Network, my second baby.

As of January, 2017, we had organised various events for a total of over five hundred women, interviewed and shared over one hundred and twenty inspirational personal stories about women as well as helped five women start their own businesses in collaboration with Ambek Investment Limited. I have also spoken at several events most of which have female audiences and have had the opportunity to inspire others to believe they can be anyone God created them to be.

Now I am sure you are wondering:

- Has the journey been smooth? Absolutely not!
- Have there been times when I had cried because things were just not going well? Yes!
- Do I still have self-doubt and fears of going broke? Yes!
- Am I always this confident? No!

- Do I let the fear and self-doubt stop me from moving forward? No! Because if I stop moving forward, then I will most definitely go completely flat-bottom broke! You see, I just keep moving with my strategy. I have plan A, B, C...up to Z. And I keep learning.

I strongly believe that women should come together to share experiences, learn, network and collaborate, hence all our activities are geared towards this course. Every woman needs a strategy for success. And for this reason, we are partnering with some of the best Business Coaches to help women strategize for success.

If you are reading this today and you know it is time for you to move on, then you need a strategy. Whether it is to focus on your own business, to find a new job, take a trip abroad or to lose weight; you need a strategy before you move. By all means, if you need help strategizing, ask for help from a Business Coach like I did. I would not advise you to simply get up and quit, have a Plan A, B, C up to Z and once you hop onto your "strategy train", just keep moving. Only take a pause to rest, think and review your strategy. Strategize and move to free yourself from the trap. Thank you.

Ama xx

Glossary

Likes - followers
P&P Newspapers - Ghanaian Newspaper
Kpakpakpa - side business
Swag - flaunt
Banku and Okro Stew Local Ghanaian dish
Besties - Best friends
Bumbum - buttocks
Fila - juicy news
Opana - term used for someone being talked about
Trotro - Mini Bus (public transport)
Tear rubber - new
Konkonsa - curious
Fanti - a tribe in Ghana
Wee-weed - urinated
Pure water - sachet water
Barney rubble - trouble
Spiritus - spiritual
Vim - confidence
Dey - present
Wahala - trouble
Kroaaa - at all
P.O.P. - Plaster of Paris

Bibliography

1. Robert Kiyosaki and Sharon Lechter, Rich Dad, Poor Dad, 1997 Warner Books Ed

2. Marianne Williamson, A Return to Love: Reflections on the Principles of "A Course in Miracles, 1993 HarperCollins

3. Yawa Hansen Quao, Daughters of Zelophehad, 2012 BlueCode Group

4. 15+ Quotes by Counsellor George Lutterodt that'll make your day, http://sasugh.blogspot.com/2016/04/15-quotes-from-counsellor-george.html

The Author

Ama Duncan is a Fabulous Child of God, Wife, Mother, Corporate Trainer, Founder of The Fabulous Woman Network (The FWN) and Corporate Training Solutions (CTS). She speaks on radio, TV shows and conferences, has been published in newspapers and blogs, and is passionate about celebrating, developing and inspiring women as well as improving service culture.

As of January, 2017, Mrs. Duncan through CTS has trained over 900 people on customer service, organized networking events and a conference for over 500 women. Through The FWN she has interviewed over 150 women and shared their inspirational stories on Facebook which has reached over 3,000,000 people in total. She is also an Access Bank W Ambassador.

Ama until April, 2016 was the Learning and Development Manager of Golden Tulip Kumasi City hotel, Ghana where her implementation of their company culture was acclaimed and recommended to other hotels. Before this, she had stints with some companies including Standard Chartered Bank (Ghana), Baylis and Harding PLC (UK), Worcestershire County Council (UK) and Camp Joy (US). She graduated from Paris Graduate School of Management, University of Ghana and Archbishop Porter

Girls' School, Ghana.

She is married to Samuel Duncan; they are blessed with Paris and Troy.

Blog: www.amaduncan.com

Email: info@thefabulouswomannetwork.com

Facebook: Ama Duncan/ The Fabulous Woman Network

Twitter: @fabwomannetwork

Instagram: The Fabulous Woman Network

Website: www.thefabulouswomannetwork.com

www.ingramcontent.com/pod-product-compliance
Lightning Source LLC
Chambersburg PA
CBHW070100100426
42743CB00012B/2612